ON TO VALHALLA!

Tristan Boyer Binns

Raintree

www.raintreepublishers.co.uk

Visit our website to find out more information about **Raintree** books.

To order:
☎ Phone 44 (0) 1865 888112
▤ Send a fax to 44 (0) 1865 314091
▭ Visit the Raintree bookshop at **www.raintreepublishers.co.uk** to browse our catalogue and order online.

First published in Great Britain by Raintree, Halley Court, Jordan Hill, Oxford OX2 8EJ, part of Harcourt Education.

Raintree is a registered trademark of Harcourt Education Ltd.

Editorial: Louise Galpine and Claire Throp
Design: Richard Parker and Tinstar Design
    www.tinstar.co.uk
Illustrations: Steve Weston, International Mapping
Picture research: Mica Brancic
Production: Julie Carter

Originated by Modern Age
Printed and bound in China by Leo Paper Group

ISBN 978 1 4062 0768 2 (hardback)
12 11 10 09 08
10 9 8 7 6 5 4 3 2 1

ISBN 978 1 4062 0775 0 (paperback)
12 11 10 09 08
10 9 8 7 6 5 4 3 2 1

British Library Cataloguing in Publication Data
Boyer Binns, Tristan
On to Valhalla!. – (Fusion)
293
A full catalogue record for this book is available from the British Library

Acknowledgements
The publishers would like to thank the following for permission to reproduce photographs: The Art Archive/Richard Wagner Museum Bayreuth/Dagli Orti (A) p. **15**; The Trustees of the British Museum p. **25**; Corbis pp. **7** (Ted Spiegel), **14** (Charles & Josette Lenars), **18** (Richard T. Nowitz), **23** (Carmen Redondo), **24** (Chris Lisle), **28** (Nik Wheeler); Corbis/ Bettmann p. **10–11**; DK Images p.**12** (Andy Crawford); Werner Forman Archive pp. **17** main pic, **27**, **29** (Statens Historiska Museum, Stockholm), **17** inset pic (Thjodminjasafn, Reykjavik, Iceland).

Cover photograph of Oseberg replica Viking ship, Norway, reproduced with permission of Getty Images/ Robert Harding World Imagery/David Lomax.

Every effort has been made to contact copyright holders of any material reproduced in this book. Any omissions will be rectified in subsequent printings if notice is given to the publishers.

The publishers would like to thank Nancy Harris and Richard Hall for their assistance with the preparation of this book.

Contents

Some words are printed in bold, **like this**. You can find out what they mean on page 30. You can also look in the box at the bottom of the page where they first appear.

With no warning

It was a summer day more than 1,200 years ago. All was quiet on an island off the north of England. The island was called Lindisfarne. (See map on page 9.) Holy men called **monks** lived on this island. They lived in a church full of treasure.

Suddenly **longships** swept to the shore. Longships were fast boats owned by Vikings. Men in helmets jumped from the boats. Their swords were drawn. The monks had no idea who their attackers were. Some monks ran away.

4

longship   fast Viking boat
monk   holy Christian man
slave   someone who is bought and sold to work without pay

The attackers took other monks to sell as **slaves**. Slaves were unpaid workers. They took treasures from the church. Then they set sail for home.

Viking fact!

Longships could go in shallow or deep water. They were good to take on oceans and rivers. Dragons were sometimes carved on the front. They looked scary!

The attack at Lindisfarne was over quickly. This was the first sign of a scary new force.

From the sea

Viking **raiders** made surprise attacks on people. They came from the countries of Denmark, Norway, and Sweden (see map on page 9).

Vikings loved to fight and sail. Viking boys learned to be **warriors** (fighters) and sailors.

Viking raids brought them glory. Raiding also brought riches. The Vikings held great feasts back at home. Poets (writers) told long stories about their brave battles.

Some Viking raiders were full-time warriors. But most were also farmers. When there was little farm work the men set sail. Their wives and children stayed home. They looked after the farm.

After a raid the Vikings sold the treasure. They also sold the **slaves** they took. The raiders shared the money they made.

Viking fact!

Vikings were not afraid to die. They believed that if you died in battle you went straight to Viking heaven.

raider someone who makes surprise attacks
warrior person who is trained to fight and do battle

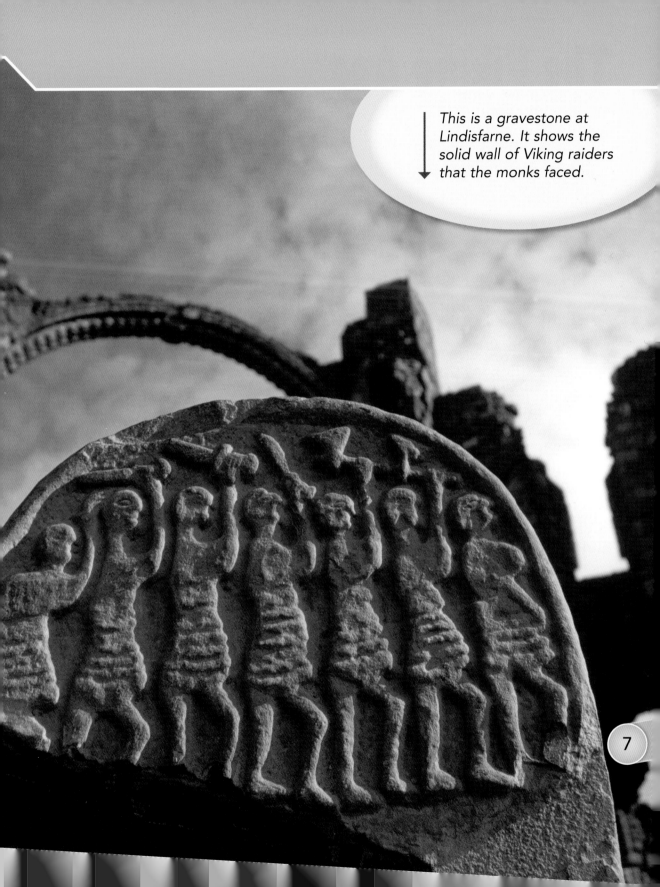

This is a gravestone at Lindisfarne. It shows the solid wall of Viking raiders that the monks faced.

The Viking Age

Vikings were very **loyal** to their leaders. This meant they followed their leaders into battle whatever happened. The leader was called a **chieftain**. A group of chieftains were loyal to a king. They followed their king into wars.

There was not enough good farmland for all the Vikings. Many Vikings went to war to win land. They settled in new places far from home.

Other Vikings loved to sail off and explore new lands. They wanted to find new places to live and get rich. Some found places where no one lived yet. Iceland and Greenland were cold, and full of ice and snow.

Some Vikings became traders. They bought and sold **goods** from all over the world. They bought goods such as silver and pottery. They sold goods such as honey and wool.

8

chieftain powerful local leader
goods things of value
loyal sticking to someone whatever happens

Viking fact!

Iceland – the name tells you how much ice there is! But there are also good places to farm. Vikings first settled there more than 1,000 years ago.

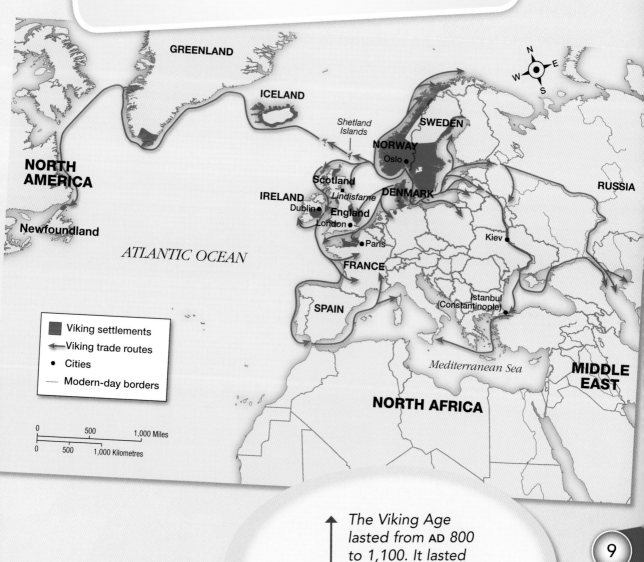

GREENLAND

ICELAND

Shetland Islands

SWEDEN

NORWAY
Oslo

NORTH AMERICA

Scotland
Lindisfarne
DENMARK

IRELAND
Dublin
England
London

RUSSIA

Kiev

Newfoundland

ATLANTIC OCEAN

Paris

FRANCE

Istanbul (Constantinople)

Viking settlements
Viking trade routes
Cities
Modern-day borders

SPAIN

Mediterranean Sea

MIDDLE EAST

NORTH AFRICA

0   500   1,000 Miles
0   500   1,000 Kilometres

The Viking Age lasted from AD 800 to 1,100. It lasted for about 300 years. The Vikings went to many faraway places.

9

Sword and shield

Vikings did not wear uniforms when raiding. Each **warrior** looked different, but all were scary!

Shields were made of wooden planks. They were shaped into a circle. An iron grip in the middle kept the warrior's hand safe. They were strong and heavy. They could bash down enemies.

Viking fact!

Swords were made from metal twisted together. The twisted metal was hammered flat. Then the edges were made very sharp.

armour   layers of tough clothes to keep the wearer safe

The more money a Viking had, the better he could protect himself. The best **armour** was made from metal. It also cost the most. Metal links were hammered together to make shirts. They were called chain mail shirts. They were hard to cut through with a sword. The poorer warriors had leather shirts and helmets.

Vikings sailed in **longships** on raids. They waited in long rows for the attack.

Raiding away!

Vikings attacked targets all over Europe. Viking **raiders** could sail their **longships** up rivers. They reached cities far from the coast this way. They even raided Paris, France (see map on page 13).

The French king was very scared of the Vikings. He paid them money to stay away. Other rulers (leaders) paid too. In England this money was known as **Danegeld**. Sometimes rulers paid so much the country had no money left. But the Vikings just attacked again.

Viking helmets never had horns. Some artists and film-makers decided they looked too plain. They added horns to make them look scarier!

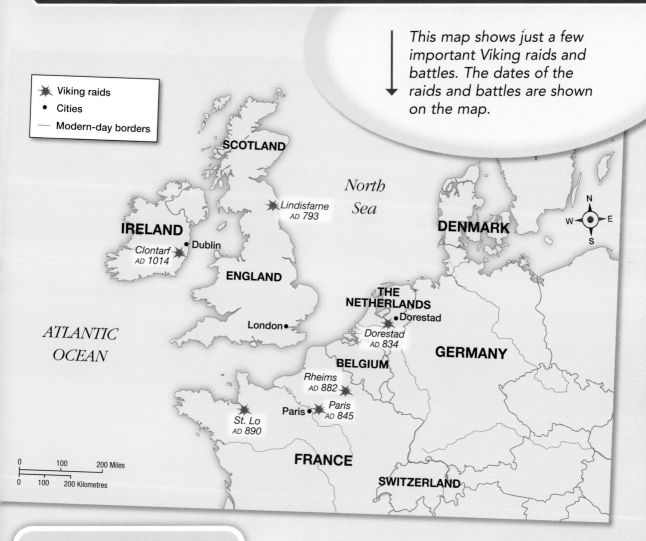

This map shows just a few important Viking raids and battles. The dates of the raids and battles are shown on the map.

Viking raids
Cities
Modern-day borders

SCOTLAND

North Sea

IRELAND

Lindisfarne AD 793

Clontarf AD 1014

Dublin

ENGLAND

DENMARK

ATLANTIC OCEAN

London

THE NETHERLANDS

Dorestad

Dorestad AD 834

GERMANY

BELGIUM

Rheims AD 882

Paris

Paris AD 845

St. Lo AD 890

FRANCE

SWITZERLAND

0   100   200 Miles
0   100   200 Kilometres

Going berserk

There were some Viking **warriors** even scarier than the rest. They were called **berserkers**. A **frenzy** took over them. It is said that they bit their shields. They also ground their teeth. They ran into battle without **armour**. Berserkers thought nothing could harm them.

Valhalla

Even the fearless Vikings died in battle. But this was not a bad thing. Vikings believed that they went to a perfect place, like heaven. This was known as an **afterlife**. For Vikings **Valhalla** was their afterlife. In Valhalla the **warriors** did battle all day. At night their wounds healed. They held a non-stop party all night long. At dawn they began fighting again.

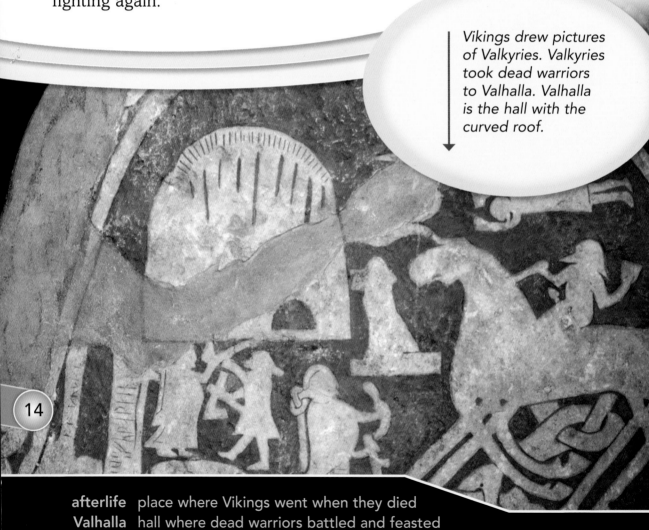

Vikings drew pictures of Valkyries. Valkyries took dead warriors to Valhalla. Valhalla is the hall with the curved roof.

afterlife   place where Vikings went when they died
Valhalla   hall where dead warriors battled and feasted
Valkyries   warrior maidens who flew to Viking battles

Viking fact!

Were there any real Viking women warriors? Some pictures show women with spears. There are stories of women on raids. Some Viking women are said to have led armies.

Artists still love to make pictures of Valkyries taking brave dead warriors to Valhalla.

15

Vikings believed in **Valkyries**. Valkyries were flying warrior women. They watched over battles on Earth. They decided who would live and who would die. Then Valkyries scooped up the fallen warriors. They flew them to Valhalla.

Viking gods

The Vikings believed in many gods and goddesses. Each one helped with something special. The Viking gods lived in a place called **Asgard**. **Valhalla** was the place where dead warriors went. It was in Asgard, too.

Odin	Odin was the most important god. He was wise and powerful. Odin sat at the head of the feasts in Valhalla.
Frigg	Frigg was Odin's wife. She was the goddess of good health and beauty.
Thor	Thor was very strong. But he was not very bright. He had a hammer. When he swung it, lightning flashed. When the hammer hit things, thunder boomed.
Frey	Frey blessed people with children. He blessed farmers with good crops (for example, corn). He had a twin sister called Freya. She was the goddess of love and death.
Loki	Loki was clever and dishonest. He was Odin's brother. He liked playing mean tricks.

Asgard home of the gods

Viking fact!

Some of the names we still use for days of the week come from Viking times. Thursday is Thor's day. Wednesday is Odin's day. Friday is named after Freya or Frigg. No one is sure which!

This is the god called Thor. He was very powerful.

Freya was the goddess of love. She later became the goddess of war and death.

17

Why in a boat?

Many brave Viking **warriors** died in battle. Many were buried where they died. Some were brought home for **funerals**. A great **chieftain** or king had an amazing funeral.

What was the best way to be buried? In a fine **longship**, of course. Viking boats meant speed and adventure. A funeral boat sped to the **afterlife**.

This burial boat was found in Gokstad, Norway. The boat is beautifully made. The man buried in it was very rich. He had three other smaller boats in the burial mound as well!

This is a photo of a bridle mount. A bridle mount is a buckle. It was part of the headgear used to control a horse.

The boat was not enough. The dead chieftain needed the same things he used when he was alive. He was dressed in his finest clothes. He had his weapons and jewellery. His funeral boat was filled with food. It also had servants and animals. Then the whole funeral boat was buried in a big mound.

Quick trip to paradise

Vikings wanted to get to the **afterlife** (heaven) quickly. They believed they could get there faster travelling in a burning boat. A traveller called Ibn Fadlan saw a Viking **chieftain's funeral**. It was in Russia. He wrote about what he saw.

This is what a Viking funeral might have looked like.